MW00848746

MOOZIE'S
COW WISDOM
For Life's Little Beefs

Best Friends Books. Breckenridge, Colorado USA

Cow Wisdom For Life's Little Beefs.

Published by Best Friends Books.

Library of Congress Catalog-in-Publication
Number 98-96010

ISBN 0-9662268-0-1

This book is Smyth-sewn to
last until the cows come home.

Illustrations by Talon Bunn
Jacket photograph by Dian McGowan

This book may be ordered from the publisher.
Please include $1.25 for postage and handling per
book. Always try your book store first.

Best Friends Books, 1-888-666-7155
P. O. Box 3880, Breckenridge, CO 80424
books@moozie.com, www.moozie.com

Who's Moozie?

Moozie is a street-smart cow who brings country wisdom to everyday life. She is no ordinary cow, for Moozie travels widely, entertaining adults and children. She looks like any other cow as she swishes her tail, nods her head and bats her eyes, until you discover she is a mechanical cow that sleeps in a suitcase.

Who's Ted Dreier?

Ted grew up on a dairy farm in Newton, Kansas. In 1969 he joined the corporate world in Dallas, Texas, later making a major lifestyle change and moving to Breckenridge, Colorado. He is the author of *Take Your Life Off Hold*. Moozie and Ted's life-mission is to spread the milk of human kindness. Let there be **moozic** in your soul. Visit moozie on the internet at www.moozie.com.

Foreword from Moozie

Some people think cows have an easy life. They forget that we are milked dry twice a day. Now don't take me wrong. We're not complaining. However, it does take work to produce milk. To produce 15 gallons of milk a day, we drink 40-50 gallons of water and eat 75-100 pounds of feed. That takes about six hours, then you add another eight hours for cud-chewing. That's a good day's work. But even with all that, we have time to think and share our wisdom.

The balanced
life is knowing
when to chew
your cud
and when
to hoof it.

Life has its
annoyances
So God gave
cows tails and
humans patience.

Negative thoughts are like fences; *they keep us from experiencing greener pastures.*

*Like cream, our
best won't come to
the top when we
are all stirred up.*

Some people treat the truth like a cow's tail, always twisting it.

Cows and
people are
remembered
for what they
give, not for
what they
consume.

Friendships and

fences need special

attention to keep

them strong.

Even cows know that if you always take the same path, you end up at the same place even cows know that if you always take the same path, you end up at the same place even cows know that if you always take the same path, you end up at the same place even cows know that if you always take the same path, you end up at the same place.

Reaping
success
and
milking
cows
takes
daily
effort.

When you
feel like crying
in your milk,
be thankful
for the milk.

When you
have been
handed
more than
you can
swallow,
**relax
and chew
your cud.**

The gate you
slam behind you
today may look
like opportunity
tomorrow.

There's more opportunity in one open gate than in ten that are closed.

Wholesome milk
and nurturing
homes build
strong children.

Today's manure produces tomorrow's greenest grass.

Watch
where you
step when
following
the herd.

Some folks
treat
personal
problems
like
manure,
spreading
them
everywhere.

COW CHIPS.

What are they? That's what is left after cows squeeze the milk out of everything they eat. On the average, cows produce 25,000 pounds of chips a year. Cow chips bring happiness to people. Jokesters make up corny jokes about them; gardeners love how they make their plants happier. Some are used for cooking and heating – and don't forget the silly cow chip throwing contests.

Gossip
is the
manure
of the
mind.

Leaders and a
bucket of milk
begin with
one little
squirt.

The demand
for sour cream
proves that
when things
turn sour there
is still hope.

Advice
and milk
make some
stronger and
give others
indigestion.

The

            greenest grass

is

found

on

the

path

least

traveled.

Cash
cows
make
**fat
cats.**

Milk attracts flies,
moo-la attracts
fly-by-nights.

Good
friends
and
good
fences
are
supportive
when
leaned
upon.

Sarcasm
and
sour milk
churn
the
stomach.

Milk and advice need
to be used before
becoming outdated.

Cows that stop
producing end up
in the meat market.

Employees that
stop producing end
up in the job market.

Today's udderly impossible ideas are tomorrow's cash cows.

Divorce is when a marriage goes from the land of milk and honey to the land of milk your honey.

Love
and
manure
do the
most
good
when
spread
around.

Maturity is taking
the bull by the
horns without
telling everyone.

Persuasion
is the act
of corralling
another's
thinking.

Irritated cows
switch their tails,

        happy dogs wag
                their tails,

and
lazy people sit on them.

When you are
having a good
time, milk
the moment
for all it's worth.

Trying to change
a person whose
mind is already
made up is as
futile as trying
to get a cow
back through
a hole in the fence.

Upset cows are

better at

holding their milk

than

upset people

are at holding

their tongues.

Two cows
mooing is noise.
When one stops
to listen, it's
cowmunication.

Meeting challenges and climbing over barbed-wire fences can be udderly painful if you don't keep on your toes.

We feel like
one of the
herd when
we are
not heard.

Ordinary
fences
are
no
obstacle
for a
person
with
moocho
gumption.

The secret
of a long life
is to keep
hoofin' it.

Risks
and
tall
fences
are
scary
only
to
those
afraid
of
falling.

There are
moovers
and shakers,
and there are
those who
need to be
shaken to
get moovin'.

Productive
people
get
up
with
the
chickens
and
keep
moooving
all
day.

Contented cows
and
contented people
are
the most productive.

Challenges,
like flies
on a cow,
can get the
best of us
if we don't
keep our tails
moooving.

Your tail
will get
stepped on
if you
stop mooovin'.

Today's

cream-of-the-crop

students

become

tomorrow's

Big Cheeses.

Taking a person
at his word or
a bull by the horns
can be an experience
long-remembered.

Expecting opportunity to knock while you do nothing is like expecting to get milk by holding out a bucket.

People and cows are most content in a stable environment.

Be yourself.
A cow that tries to act
like a horse doesn't
have good cow sense.

Jumping to conclusions and jumping over a barbed-wire fence can be udderly disastrous.

Today's lazy cows become tomorrow's meat loaf.

Winners and losers often are on the same path, but *winners keep mooovin'*.

It's impossible for people and cows to give their best when bogged down in barnyard muck.

Worrying and a
swinging cow's
tail takes energy
which doesn't
move you forward.

When
you
follow
the
herd
the
view
never
changes.

Building a close
relationship and
milking a cow
are difficult from
a distance.

Milking a
topic dry
is udderly
boring.

Folks
get
sore
when
others
horn
in.

God gave cows
two horns to
get attention
and humans
two ears to
pay attention.

MOOZIE REFLECTION:
Motorists driving in the country often stop to watch us cows. We enjoy the attention. Watching cows is better than watching TV – especially if you want to get to the land of milk and honey. Why? Because in the Bible cows are mentioned 44 times and TV not once.

Lead cows

     have
     the
     freshest
     view
     and
     are
     the
     first
     to
     step
     off
     the
     edge.

Talking
to a
narrow-minded
person is
like trying
to get a
stubborn cow
into the barn.

Folks

who are

always chewing

the fat become broader.

Cows and shoppers
know that some brands
take more out of your
hide than others.

Friendships and cows' tails are sorely missed when gone.

A cow pasture
and
a child's
unkempt bedroom
have evidence
of dumping.

Cowfucius say: Person with chip on shoulder dump on others.

Don't
count
on
being
bailed
out
when
things
                are
going
                    haywire.

When cows or people
have their tails in
the air, you know
someone is going to
get dumped on.

*Sitting in church
doesn't make
you any
holier than
sitting in a
barn makes
you a cow.*

A cow's security
is knowing she can
get back in through
the same hole in the
fence she came out.

Praying for help and doing nothing is like expecting a cow to give milk by just asking.

Be careful
whom
you
follow,
for
many
a cow
has
followed
the herd
into the
butcher's
truck.

Fences and stomachs need tightening to keep them from sagging.

People who always shoot the bull seldom grab the bull by the horns.

Butter comes from
churning milk;
butterflies come from
churning stomachs.

Take-home-pay
and skim milk have
the fat removed.

Telling a blabber-mouth a secret is like milking a cow into a leaky bucket.

*Feelings are
the cream
of rich
relationships.*

*A life without
hope is like a fence
without a gate.*

Don't wait
until the
cows come home
to say
I love you.